God's People at Worship

Young

*Very young children
in all-age worship*

Judy Jarvis

*Jointly published by
Division of Education and Youth
and
Methodist Publishing House*

First published April 1995

© Methodist Church Division of Education and Youth

ISBN 0 7192 0195 0
ISBN 1 85852 041 X
Illustrations: Helen Mahood

Jointly published by
Methodist Church Division of Education and Youth
2 Chester House, Pages Lane, London N10 1PR
and
Methodist Publishing House
20 Ivatt Way, Peterborough PE3 7PG

Printed by
Clifford Frost Limited, Lyon Road,
Windsor Avenue, London SW19 2SE

God's People at Worship

An introduction to the series

'God's People at Worship' is a series of booklets about Christian worship, particularly when all ages are involved.

For simplicity, the phrase *all-age worship* is used throughout the series, despite its shortcomings. The word *worship* should need no qualification. In worship, people offer themselves – with all their similarities and differences (including their ages) – to God. Unfortunately, *worship* has come to be seen as a mainly adult activity. To describe it as *all-age* provides a useful reminder that it is the business of the whole people of God.

The booklets in the series deal with different aspects of all-age worship. The emphasis is mainly practical, looking at *How?* questions. However, *Why?* questions are also dealt with, particularly in the introductory volume, *One*.

'God's People at Worship' is for worship leaders; for those who plan, prepare and co-ordinate worship in local churches; for workers with children and young people; for church musicians; for people who are creative in written or spoken word, dance, drama or visual arts; for stewards, members of worship consultations and Church Councils and all those who make decisions about the church's worship. But, above all, our hope is that these booklets will be read and used by Christian people of all ages who care about worship.

Young, the ninth in the series, considers the place of children under seven in all-age worship. Should they be there at all? If so, what can be done to help them feel welcome and involved? *Young* takes seriously both the needs of young children and the concerns of those who worship with them.

'God's People at Worship' is produced jointly by the Methodist Publishing House and the Division of Education and Youth, in consultation with representatives of the Division of Ministries and the Worship Commission.

The General Editor of the series is Rev. David Gamble, working with an Advisory Group (Mrs Judy Jarvis, Rev. John Lampard, Mr Brian Sharp and Mr Brian Thornton).

Contents

1	At the beginning	7
2	All together	9
3	Setting the scene	12
4	Music making	17
5	Our Father, who art in heaven...'	27
6	A book full of stories	33
7	Once upon a time...	36
8	Acting it out	40
9	Hosanna, Hallelujah	44
10	Where two or three...	47
11	The Lord bless you and keep you...	49
12	The bread we break	54
13	The Kingdom of God belongs to such as these	59
14	Resources	61

1 At the beginning

It was the first Sunday of Advent. The village congregation was gathered for the monthly Family Service. All ages were present, from small babies, through toddlers and young children to elderly members who had been there every Sunday for longer than they cared to remember.

In the vestry the young Local Preacher with whom I was to lead the service quietly breastfed her baby, 'topping him up' before the service began.

At the front of the church, where the choir used to sit, was an area without pews. It contained a low table, small chairs, books, toys, paper, felt tipped pens and other items of interest to small children. During the service children moved freely and quietly from their family groups to their special area and back again.

The theme of the service was Light and Darkness. As I described my visit to Belfast a few days before, the children came to sit on the floor at my feet. Instead of becoming increasingly fidgety as the service progressed, they became quieter and quieter, more and more absorbed.

The service ended with prayers. Everyone lit small candles from a central candle. Older children lit their own. Parents lit candles for their small babies. This was not a church where anyone could be left out.

This booklet is about young children in worship. It is about worship that is truly 'all-age', not worship where all those under three, under five, or under seven, have been quietly removed. It is about rejoicing in the advantages and opportunities, while facing the problems and difficulties. It recognizes that many of the perceived problems are not created by children, but by adults, whether worship leaders, decision-makers within the church, or members of the worshipping community.

2 All together

'How can we worship with toddlers running up and down the aisle?' 'Children fidgeting at the front are a distraction.' 'Crying babies should be taken out.'

Such questions and comments are familiar. Some reflect prejudice. Others, perhaps, contain the ring of truth. Why indeed, should we 'put up' with young children in church?

There is, of course, a great dilemma. We want to affirm that everyone is of equal value in the sight of God, regardless of gender, colour or age. We also recognize that worship lies at the heart of the Christian community and plays an essential part in our relationship with God. The corollary of this is that worship is for everyone.

Herein lies the dilemma. How can everyone worship together when there is such a range of needs and interests? Should not the younger children be excluded to help adults to 'cope' better? How can we reconcile principles and practice?

Human development in the first seven years of life is far greater than in any other period. Obviously **children under three** are limited in their ability to participate in worship. They are, however, aware of being in an environment where they are loved and cared for. They can share a sense of wonder at things going on around them.

Between three and five remarkable progress is made. Language develops, along with the ability to join in songs and hymns, take part in prayers and listen to stories, although the attention span is very short.

Children of five to seven can do all these things. They can also both ask and answer perceptive questions. They can make a valuable contribution, if they are allowed to!

The challenge is to create a worshipping environment in which young children are welcomed and involved but which is not a dilution of all that we value in worship. There are times, of course, when it is right and proper to worship separately, but this does not remove the responsibility to ensure that worship is rich and meaningful when all ages, including the very youngest, gather together.

How welcome a young child actually feels depends largely on the members of the congregation. Do adults chat enthusiastically to friends before worship begins and then disapprove if children talk? Do door stewards welcome children in their own right or do they welcome parents and neglect the children? During coffee after the service are the children included or are they left to run around, bored, longing to go home?

The service of worship is not held in isolation. It is potentially the high moment when the members of the church community meet with God. Good relationships within that community will significantly affect the quality of the worship, and will help people of all ages know they belong.

3   Setting the scene

The setting in which worship takes place is very important. If parents are frantically trying to keep squirming toddlers on their laps because there is nowhere for them to go, there is bound to be disruption. Where there is no crèche, sooner or later a baby's crying will obliterate the sermon – perhaps no bad thing, in some cases! Three to five year olds crammed together on a pew are likely to chat, push and shove. In smaller numbers they may discover that seat cushions slide beautifully from one end of the pew to the other.

Special areas for the very young

Some churches have removed a few pews and made a special carpeted area with a low table, bean bags and chairs for children (or parents) to sit on. Books, games, drawing materials and carefully chosen toys are essentials. Avoid rattles and other noisy toys, like small cars that depend on sound for maximum effect. Toys should be spotlessly clean and in good repair. Too often the toys available to children in church are castoffs, and look like it.

There are many lovely children's books. Some libraries provide them on extended loan. If not, good quality paperbacked picture books, regularly replaced, are infinitely preferable to tired second-hand books that have seen better days. Low shelves allow books and toys to be easily available and attractively displayed. Bright pictures, low enough for children to see, should be changed regularly. If the First Steps or Cradle Roll is displayed here, young children are soon able to pretend that they recognize their names on it, having been shown a few times. An album with photographs taken at baptisms is often a great attraction and can be placed here too.

Churches with chairs rather than pews have very little problem in setting up such an area, given the will. It is a great temptation, however, to do this only for Family Services. Children need to feel that they have their own special part of the church, not something which is used as an expedient to keep them quiet when it suits the adults.

Some churches create a 'cage' of chairs within which parents and very young children can sit. This gives freedom to move around and play with toys, but avoids children disappearing into the pulpit. It is obviously an inferior solution to the creation of a special children's area, but is better than nothing. It encourages not only the children, but, importantly, their parents, who frequently worry about their children's behaviour and about how other adults react.

Some churches have a soundproofed screen behind which parents and young children can sit, with a loudspeaker relaying the service. This may seem an ideal solution, enabling children and parents to relax. But do they feel part of the worshipping community or like spectators at a play? To what extent are the rest of the congregation escaping their responsibilities and opportunities for fellowship?

Crèches

The traditional way of providing for very young children has been to run a crèche in a separate room. Too often, however, this has been staffed by young teenagers. The facilities have been limited to one box of grubby broken toys and parents have been made to feel guilty if they refuse to leave their child. A well-run crèche needs proper care and preparation. Plan the facilities carefully, making sure that the leadership is stable (the same each week if possible). Give parents the opportunity to choose whether to use it or not.

Furniture and Equipment

Many churches replace pews with chairs chosen only with adults in mind. Young children can slip off them, fall through the backs, or tip them over. The consequent yells and screams are easy to imagine.

Sometimes churches save money by carpeting only certain areas, perhaps inside the communion rail and up the central aisle. Carpeting the whole church, where possible, makes it much quieter when young children move around and much more pleasant for babies and toddlers, who spend a lot of time sitting or crawling on the floor.

Hopefully, the days are gone when ancient hymn-books with pages missing were reserved for children. Nevertheless, it is common to see books only provided for children old enough to read. Younger children love to be helped to find the place in their own book, even if they sometimes hold it upside down! The considerable risk of books being dropped is surely preferable to children feeling 'left out'.

General atmosphere

As a bridesmaid of barely three years old, I remember vividly the dress of the adult bridesmaid who accompanied me down the aisle. It was a vivid deep orange/peach and it felt wonderful. Later I learned that it was made of velvet. I also remember, at a very early age, visiting a great cathedral, and being entranced by the wonderful sounds coming from the organ. Young children are very sensitive to their surroundings. They can appreciate beauty long before they can express their feelings in any depth. As with adults, it is through their senses that young children learn about the world in which they live.

We need to consider this when we think about the church environment into which we bring young children. It is important that the church is kept in good repair, with things to look at - whether a simple central cross, or bright banners. Children instinctively understand which things are valued by the adults around them. A cold, dingy and unwelcoming building can create barriers that have to be overcome in other ways.

How the church looks is only part of the impact on young children. Equally important are sounds, whether of beautiful music or friendly voices. Vital also, is the chance for them to smell the flower arrangement if they wish (despite the possible horror of the flower arranger), to touch some of the things around them and to grasp a welcoming hand.

Patently, there are many examples of cases when the worship has been such that the setting has paled into insignificance, but this does not absolve us from the responsibility to do all we can to make churches places of welcome to young children.

4 Music making

'Born in song!
God's people have always been singing.
Born in song!
Hearts and voices raised.
So today we worship together;
God alone is worthy to be praised.'

© *Brian Hoare and Jubilate Hymns.*

Singing

Even unborn children can appreciate music. Certainly, before the age of two, young children can join in 'Postman Pat, Postman Pat, and his black and white cat'.

The easiest form of music for young children to copy is the human voice, particularly the female voice, which is nearer in pitch. As long as the singer is in tune, the quality of the voice is immaterial.

We often 'write off' young children when we sing during worship, with hymns whose words and tune are too difficult, even for those who are beginning to read. Then we let them sing their own song and respond as an appreciative audience to 'If I were a butterfly' or 'I love the sun, he shines on me'. In fact, there is much music in which all ages can share and sharing songs brings a great feeling of togetherness.

Responsive songs

Songs using a cantor and response (if a volunteer cantor can be found), overcome two hurdles for young children – they can copy, easily, both the tune and the words. Here are two examples:

He Came Down

© From **Many & Great**, World Church Songs, Vol 1. (Wild Goose Publications).
Arrangement: Copyright 1990 Iona Community, Glasgow, Scotland.
Used by permission.

Gloria
(shortened)

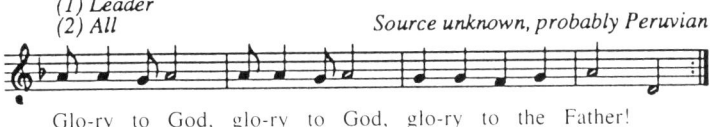

2. Glory to Christ Jesus
3. Glory to the Spirit

Songs with simple words

Some songs are written especially for children. Others have simple words which convey very important truths. It is delightful to hear young children singing them but they should never be used as songs for everyone to join in. 'If I were a butterfly' can become merely a parody when sung by a forty-seven year-old bank manager or a young person in leathers, and, incidentally, would be extremely unpopular with most children over the age of seven or eight.

Simple well-known songs for everybody to sing include 'Kum ba ya' (Hymns and Psalms (HP) 525) and 'He's got the whole world in his hand' (HP 25).

The World Church is a rich source of material. The Iona Community's books, *Many and Great* and *Sent by the Lord,* have many good examples, including:

Halle, Halle, Halle

From *Many & Great*, World Church Songs Vol. 1 (Wild Goose Publications).
Arrangement: © 1990 Iona Community, Glasgow, Scotland. Used by permission.

Story Song also contains some songs suitable for all ages, including the youngest. These include: 'Little Zacchaeus had tax fraud fame', 'In the Beginning' and 'Sanna, Sannanina'.

© *1993 Stainer & Bell Ltd. and Methodist Church Division of Education and Youth. Reproduced from <u>Story Song</u>.*

Rounds

'Frere Jacques' and 'London's burning' are favourites with young children. The use of simple rounds for all ages together brings a challenge and sense of achievement (usually!). The following are fairly foolproof:

> Seek ye first the kingdom of God (HP 138)
> Father, we adore you (Junior Praise 44)
> The Lord is my Shepherd, I'll trust him always (Junior Praise 244)

Songs with actions

Approach these with great care. Countless adults have been put off Family Services for life by being asked to sing, and act out, 'Stand up, clap hands, shout thank you Lord'! Young children love songs with actions, but can be helped to understand that many adults are more inhibited. Adults may learn gradually the fun of doing more than merely singing and may, for example, join in clapping out a strong rhythm to a song.

Creating songs

Young children can lead a congregation in creating something new, opening possibilities for the older people around them.

O, What a Wonderful World

2. O what a beautiful world!
O what a beautiful world it is!
O what a beautiful world!
Thank you, my Lord Jesus.

3. O what a marvellous world!
O what a marvellous world it is!
O what a marvellous world!
Thank you, my Holy Spirit.

© *Copyright by Kevin Mayhew Ltd.*
Used by permission from Good Morning, Jesus Licence Number 496030

This song is very easy to learn. Children (and others) can choose suitable adjectives for following verses to replace 'wonderful'. 'Beautiful' and 'marvellous' are obvious examples, but words which do not scan should not be rejected. 'Fantastic' becomes a challenge. (Adults are more likely than children to come up with 'supercallafragalistic-expialidocious'!)

Suggestions such as 'sad, unhappy world' should of course be affirmed and sung, perhaps changing the final line to 'Help us, Heavenly Father'.

'Grown-up' hymns

Just as adults enjoy a varied diet of music, so do young children. They will love to join in some 'big' hymns of the faith with good strong tunes, even though the words will be

beyond their understanding. A childhood favourite of mine was 'Thy hand, O God, has guided' sung to 'Thornbury'. It is a mistake never to stretch a child's (or an adult's) horizons.

Playing

Young children enjoy playing percussion instruments. Under 7s normally use unpitched instruments, whether home-made or bought. The chance to play an instrument during worship provides a valuable opportunity for participation, but it should not be abused. Weekly accompaniment becomes routine and ordinary to the children, and something to be endured for the adults. It may be better for two or three children to take it in turns to accompany the singing than for the whole group to take part at once.

Listening

There is seldom much opportunity to listen to music during worship. Organ voluntaries are often drowned by conversation or by the sound of people leaving. Some churches have choirs. Others make space during worship to listen to a soloist, group, or pre-recorded music. Very often this happens after the children have left the service. In fact, they enjoy and benefit from the chance to listen quietly, in a world dominated by activity and visual images, as long as it is not for too long.

Dance and movement

Very young children find it difficult to move in precise time to music or to remember sequences of steps. On the other hand, they love a good excuse to get out of their seats and to move around. It is adults who are less willing to take part. One way of overcoming the problem is to ask everyone to move for a purpose, such as carrying and waving palm branches on Palm Sunday.

5 Our Father, who art in heaven . . .

Young children can pray very naturally. Many children around the age of four or five have an unseen friend who plays an important part in their lives and accompanies them everywhere. It is but a short step for them to talk to God.

It is easy to give the impression that the one place to talk to God is in church and that it has to be done in a particular way, by expert adults, to be valid. To approach prayer in a variety of ways demonstrates that there is no one, 'proper', way to pray.

Creating the right atmosphere for prayer is particularly helpful to young children. This may sometimes involve the use of candles, music, symbols, or the quiet bringing forward of gifts. 'Finger writing' on slips of paper (to preserve anonymity and to help those who cannot write) is a good way of confessing sins, or, in the terms of young children, thinking of things about which they are sorry. The papers can be collected and burnt in a suitable container.

Sometimes worship leaders over-compensate for the presence of young children. Saying 'Hands together, eyes closed' separates children from everyone else. Incidentally, it also signals to the adults that they need not listen, as this is a prayer for children. Similarly, phrases such as 'God bless our mummies and daddies' single out children. Prayer must be able to be offered by everyone present.

Children's attitudes are established at a very early age and careful thought should be given as to how to address God. It is common, particularly when children are present, to

address God as 'Father'. However, some children's image of 'father' may be very unhappy, or they may have no father to whom they can relate. The description of God as Father should go alongside others, such as Creator, Friend, Mother.

Prayers from the Liturgy

Young children love nursery rhymes. They have very retentive memories. They love to roll long words off their tongues. Most five and six year olds know more names of dinosaurs than do adults. We should not be afraid to use some of the great traditional prayers, particularly, of course, the Lord's Prayer. Regular use encourages children to learn them and join in repeating them. They do not need to understand every word (how many adults do?). What matters is sharing in something of significance to those around them.

Extempore Prayer

This can be the most difficult type of prayer to use with young children present (or perhaps at any time!). The prayer must not be too long and must be well thought out, avoiding obscure theological concepts or language. However, carefully used, extempore prayer can be appropriate.

Responsive Prayer

Prayers with a response can hold young children's attention and provide an opportunity to join in. When and how to respond need to be clearly explained. The response could be repeated twice at the outset – for the benefit of everyone.

Young children can quickly pick up simple sung responses, such as 'O Lord hear my prayer'. (See page 30.)

Intercessions

Many churches invite suggestions of people for whom to pray. Children's suggestions must be taken seriously, even if it is tempting to feel that the health of Simon's budgerigar is of a somewhat different order from Mrs Smith's terminal cancer or floods in Bangladesh.

Prayers with a simple structure

Some profound prayers have a very simple structure which enables them to be more easily understood. Many Celtic prayers come in this category:

Come Lord
Come down
Come in
Come among us
Come as the wind
To move us
Come as the light
To prove us
Come as the night
To rest us
Come as the storm
To test us
Come as the sun
To warm us
Come as the stillness
To calm us
Come Lord
Come down
Come in
Come among us.

By David Adam from Tides and Seasons, *1989. Used by permission of the publishers, SPCK.*

and

The Lord is here,
The Lord is there,
The Lord is everywhere.
The Lord is high,
The Lord is low,
The Lord is on the path I go.

By David Adam from Tides and Seasons, *1989. Used by permission of the publishers, SPCK.*

Children's own prayers

Often children are asked to write their own prayers and read them. This can become a performance rather than a prayer. Frequently, young children become very shy and cannot be heard. It is infinitely preferable if people of different ages prepare prayers, rather than singling out children. (Adults may also realize what a difficult task has been set.)

Silent prayer

If others around them are praying silently, small children will usually do the same. The silence, of course, must not be too long. Occasionally a very small child will take the opportunity to exercise the vocal chords, delighting in the unaccustomed attention. In these circumstances the worship leader may decide to curtail the silence somewhat sooner than intended.

6 A book full of stories

It may not always be appropriate to have the Bible readings while young children are present in worship. If they are leaving to share with their own age group it may be more suitable for them to hear from the Bible within that group. On the other hand, it is very important that, from an early age, children begin to understand that the Bible is central to worship and matters a great deal to everyone around them. This is a strong argument for all ages listening together.

Use of translations

The *Good News Bible* is a good translation for general use with all ages. Other translations are worth consideration for specific passages. The first chapter of John's gospel, read in the beautiful language of the *Authorized Version* at a Christmas Carol Service, cannot be surpassed.

Many 'Children's Bibles' are neither suitable to give to children nor to use in worship. The content of some is excessively sentimental. Some purport to be written for children but with little idea of what is appropriate. Some are theologically unsound. Some are not intended for reading to a large group. Of a very different order, are Alan Dale's versions of the Old and New Testaments, *Winding Quest* and *New World*. A. J. McCallen's *Praise* was written with very young children in mind, but in a way that enriches the experience of all ages. These words are from Psalm 139:

You know me, Lord, so very well,
you know when I get up.
You know when I go back to sleep,
you know each thing I do.

You know what I am going to say
before I even speak!
You are always close to me.
You're wonderful, O Lord.

So if I climb the highest hill,
you would be there with me.
And if I swam beneath the waves,
you'd still be there with me.

Even in the dark at night
you would be next to me.
Yes, even then I could not hide,
you would be there with me.

From Praise, *by A.J. McCallen published by HarperCollins Religious, an imprint of HarperCollins Publishers.*

Consideration of content

Some parts of the Bible are much easier to understand than others. The epistles, for instance, are difficult for five year olds, but they can begin to understand many gospel passages. The Old Testament seems to contain many rattling good stories for children, but it is important to maintain balance. It is difficult to help young children to think of a loving, caring God if they are brought up on a diet of vengeance and conflict. Two favourite stories for young children, Noah and the flood, and David and Goliath, come into this category.

Dramatized reading

This is now much easier to organize, following the publication of *The Dramatised Bible,* though many groups have been preparing their own readings for years. Using several voices immediately adds interest, especially for small children. It may be possible to involve five and six year olds but take care not to make them feel vulnerable about their reading ability. It is also necessary, usually, to provide a microphone – at the right level – and plenty of time to rehearse.

Use of copies

Five and six year olds enjoy following a Bible reading along with everyone else. They are seldom provided with copies. A Bible of the translation normally used in the church makes a good presentation gift at a Baptism or when a child moves to a different group within the Junior Church. Young children can delight in arriving at church armed with their 'own' Bible.

7 Once upon a time...

Telling stories is an intrinsic part of our human nature. We do it all the time. The power of story crosses all age-groups. A good story will absorb three year olds to ninety-three year olds. Children under three enjoy stories too, but need to share them on a one-to-one basis. On some occasions their attention span will be very short. On other occasions they will want the story again and again and again!

Telling stories

The traditional 'Children's Address' was often a time for telling a story. Many an adult has emerged from a service, including a twenty-minute sermon, with vivid memories of the Children's Address and little else.

A good story, well-told, has an enormous impact. There are also some pitfalls.

- A story should stand by itself. The minute the 'moral' is attached everyone switches off, especially the children.
- There should always be a valid reason for telling a story – to amuse the young ones is not enough.
- The story needs to be known well to the story-teller and practised, so that eye contact can be maintained.
- Young children respond particularly well to stories which are told, rather than read.

- Care should be taken not to confuse fact and fiction. Enough problems have been caused by linking the arrival of Father Christmas with the birth of Jesus.

Reading stories

Some stories have been so well written that it would be an insult to try to improve on the original. But stories which are to be read should be practised in advance.

Bible stories

Bible stories are so regularly read that it often helps people to a new understanding when they are told. It is also an opportunity to 'pad-out' some of the 'one-liners' of Jesus to give them extra meaning and impact. A good example of this principle, written specifically for young children is *The Little Gate* by Butterworth and Inkpen.

What other stories?

In addition to the Bible there is a wide range of Christian literature, often well produced and illustrated. The written content is not always so good. Many books can be used in worship and will have an impact on a wide age-range, including young children. For example, ideas and illustrations can be taken from C S Lewis' *Narnia* Series, *I am David* by Anne Holm, *The Velveteen Rabbit* by Marjorie Williams, or *Badger's Parting Gifts* by Susan Varley. Books which could, in certain circumstances, be read in their entirety or with some amendment include Oscar Wilde's *The Selfish Giant* or *The Happy Prince*, *The Clown of God* by Tomie de Paola, and *Babylon* by Jill Paton Walsh.

Use of humour

This is not a plea for the 'a funny thing happened to me on the way to the church' approach, but a recognition that laughter crosses age barriers and builds relationships. It touches deeper feelings and enables the sharing of sadness as well as joys. But children's humour and adult humour can be very different. Children are very perceptive to what is forced and artificial. It is necessary to be sensitive to their responses.

Use of poetry

Children's love of rhythm and words has already been mentioned. Young children love poetry (a love which is sometimes obliterated in later years by the attitude of the adults around them). In addition, a poem may say in a few words what might have taken a whole sermon – a distinct advantage in the context of all-age worship. The following poem for instance, will be understood by children and adults, from their own perspectives.

> God made me
> And I made a sandcastle
> A model aeroplane and a car.
> God made me and I made friends
> With Ann and James and Tim.
> God made me and gave
> me his power to make things.
> God made me to go on with
> what he began.

Anon, 10 years.
(Reproduced from Fresh Voices *with the permission of the National Christian Education Council.)*

Telling our own stories

It can be very helpful to share our own experiences, as long as they are used in context, to illuminate the central purpose of the worship, and to bring deeper understanding to children, young people and adults. Young children (and indeed all ages) enjoy vivid descriptions of childhood experiences which enable the hearer to identify with the teller.

Children telling their own stories

Never force children to tell their own stories, but encourage them to do so. It may sometimes be necessary to encourage them to stop! Both the leader of worship and the members of the congregation need to be sensitive. It is easy to laugh at what a young child has said and cause, unintentionally, considerable distress.

8 Acting it out

It is the great day of Pentecost. All ages are gathered to celebrate. The reading of Acts 2 begins. From different parts of the church comes the sound of a mighty wind as large pieces of cardboard are shaken, accompanied by long 'shshsh' noises. At the mention of tongues of flame, long orange, red and yellow strips of crêpe paper are waved in the air. People of all ages, including the very young, are celebrating the coming of the Spirit.

Young children respond to drama created by others, but of far greater value is that in which they are involved themselves. Too frequently we remember this, but see their contribution as a performance to the adult audience. The Christmas Nativity Play is the best-known example. We expect the children's performance to conform to our own expectations. Young children dress up in dressing-gowns and tea-towels and are sorted out by anxious adults. The temporary shepherds look very self-conscious and often have no idea why they are dressed so strangely and given a long stick to hold. I well remember a young 'shepherd' spending the whole of a service pointing his crook at me in a menacing fashion and going 'bang, bang'.

Young children can be involved in groups of different ages working together to bring Bible stories, other stories, thoughts and feelings alive through drama. Children under seven will only be able to take a very limited responsibility for initiating ideas but they will follow the lead of others with great enthusiasm.

Spontaneous drama

Every time the Lord's Supper is re-enacted in a Service of Holy Communion it is, in a sense, a drama in which everyone plays a part. But there are other ways to involve everyone, including the very young. People can march up the aisle during a psalm of approach. On Ash Wednesday last year's palm crosses can be burned and the ashes used to make crosses on the foreheads of everyone present. On Palm Sunday all the members of the congregation can join a procession or wave branches during the appropriate hymn. On the Sunday before Christmas children and adults can make Christingles during the service and walk in procession to place them round the communion rail.

Following a narrative

One very effective way of bringing a narrative alive is to create 'instant' drama. Volunteers are required, and, after a short explanation, the narrator begins. The instructions are built into the script. This has been very successfully done to illustrate the story of John Wesley being plucked as 'a brand from the burning'. The 'props' included a stacked table and chairs from which John was rescued. Volunteers of all ages took the parts of Samuel Wesley (John's father), Hetty (his sister), the nursemaid, John's brothers and sisters, two rescuers and some crowd members.

> *(John, his brothers and sisters and the nursemaid were all draped over the chairs 'asleep' and Samuel Wesley was sitting on a chair alongside reading.)*

The narrator began:

> Between eleven and twelve o'clock on a cold February night Hetty, John's sister, was awoken by sparks of fire falling on her bed. The roof of the old rectory was on fire. Samuel Wesley, John's father, rushed to the nursery, waking the nursemaid and telling her to get the children out into the garden. She snatched up the youngest and told the other children to follow. All the children did except for young John who was five years old. He only awoke

when all the rest of the family was in the garden. Mr Wesley counted his children and found one missing. Then he heard a cry from the upstairs room and knew it was John. Several times he tried to get up to him but the stairs were ablaze. Mr Wesley thought he had lost his son and began praying to God. People from the crowd saw there was no time to be lost. They lifted one of the lighter men on to the shoulders of someone else and just as the burning roof crashed in they reached John down.

Father Samuel was so happy that all his children were safe that he said: 'Come, neighbours, let us kneel down! Let us give thanks to God! He has given me all my children: let the house go, I am rich enough!'

This kind of drama can also be done following a small amount of previous preparation. Some examples of particular appeal to under-sevens are given in *Noah's Ark* by Bride Adams-Ray.

Mime

At its finest mime is a supreme, subtle art which, at its simplest level, can involve all ages. A group can choose a parable or other Bible story and make it come alive after 20 to 30 minutes sharing together. (Longer than this and they seek for perfection and start getting scared!) Sometimes groups choose to perform while a narrator reads the story. Sometimes the mime speaks for itself. The range of suitable Bible stories is endless, but it is better to retell a short story rather than a very long one. Stories such as The Lost Coin (Luke 15.8-10), The Good Samaritan (Luke 10.30-37) and Moses in the Bulrushes (Exodus 2.1-10) are useful starting points.

Performing a play

It is great fun and a good experience for a group to prepare a play for performance during worship, especially if the group develops its own script. Make sure, however, that there are sufficient rehearsals for the final result to be creditable within the context of worship. Too often churches 'make do' with second best. Children are accustomed to high standards at school and it is sad when they see what happens at church as 'second-rate'.

Drama offers a great opportunity for the congregation to participate in worship in different ways. They may rock from side to side to experience the storm on the Sea of Galilee or merely watch others. Whichever they do, there is a chance that they will look at the story with new eyes.

9 Hosanna, Hallelujah

Festivals would, at first sight, seem the most obvious occasions for young children to be present in worship. They are, after all, times when the whole family wishes to be together. However, they are sometimes the very occasions when the church community is split up - perhaps to enable the adults to celebrate 'in peace'?

Christmas

It is taken for granted that children will be present for the Nativity Play and on Christmas morning. On those occasions young children are in the foreground. They are often less welcome at the Carol Service, despite all the trappings: the tree, the candles, the dimmed lights, the music. What can be done to make them feel welcome everywhere?

Palm Sunday

The inhibitions of adults can often be overcome by the enthusiasm of young children to wave palm branches and celebrate. It is less easy to help the young children to any real understanding of the significance of Holy Week. Should we even try? But, is it possible for them to experience the joy of Easter without some of the pain of Good Friday?

Good Friday

Many adults feel very strongly that a Good Friday service is not the place for young children. This, surely, depends on the nature of the service. At one Good Friday service the children spent the time making an Easter garden with plants, flowers, turfs and rocks. On Easter Day they really had something to celebrate!

Pentecost

On this, the birthday of the church, everyone should have the opportunity to celebrate, perhaps by creating and bringing forward symbols of the Spirit: Fire, Wind and Dove. These help to bring alive a concept which can be difficult for adults as well as children.

Of course, on a birthday, a birthday cake is always appropriate.

Harvest

Many children are familiar with harvest at school as well as at church. Bringing forward their gifts gives them a guaranteed part to play (though it is important to have some 'spares' for those who have come unprepared). The relevance of a Harvest Festival in an urban society is often questioned. At the least it is necessary to try to anticipate what young children may not understand because of their lack of relevant experience. Why is the bread such a funny shape? What is a sheaf of wheat? What is wheat? What has bread got to do with wheat anyway?

Junior Church Festival/Sunday School Anniversary

This is still the occasion, in many churches, when children are expected to perform to an audience of adults. Whether it is an occasion for worship is sometimes debatable. At its best, it may be. At less than its best it is the responsibility of the worshipping community to question the way forward. What occasion might the whole church celebrate together, affirming the importance of everyone within it?

Church Anniversary

The annual Church Anniversary can be a time when the whole church community celebrates its life together. One church, each year, lays a huge painting of a tree with roots and branches in the centre of the worship area. Different people then recount the church's story, standing in the appropriate place on the tree; from the oldest people (the roots), through the active people in the life of the church (the trunk) to the branches and twigs (the children and young people). This kind of celebration would not be suitable everywhere, but shows how one church has looked seriously at the contribution of all ages.

10   Where two or three . . .

'We're only a small church.' 'We've only a few children.' 'We can't offer what the big churches can.' 'We haven't enough leadership.' 'We haven't enough money.'

The problems of small churches, many of them in rural areas, are well known and often seem to outweigh the advantages. Older children, for instance, need the support of a group of peers which small churches are often unable to provide. No such problem occurs for smaller children, who need a loving, supporting, caring community. Small size, both in buildings and numbers, is an asset. Young children can get to know everybody and feel at home. This has several positive effects.

Very young children are much less fractious if they feel comfortable in their surroundings. If they feel relaxed and happy their parents and the other adults around will respond in similar fashion. This, in turn, has a further good influence upon the young child.

Children of two and three are often frightened by a large building and crowds of people. Their experience is of home and family. They have not yet encountered the large assembly hall of a school and the hurly-burly of the playground. A small chapel with a small congregation can enable them to participate in worship without feeling daunted. And a three year old dropping the collection plate seldom causes too much chaos and distress.

Most rural and small churches are based within their local community, where everybody knows one another (or at least they know neighbours better than in many other situations).

This, again, is a huge benefit for young children who need the constant reinforcement of familiarity.

It was no accident that the first chapter in this booklet described the experience in a small country chapel, which ten years before had consisted of a few elderly ladies and had been doomed to close. The arrival of one or two young families into the village and into the life of the chapel was the catalyst needed. The families could not be made fully welcome unless attitudes changed, to each other, and to worship. Changes took place. A children's area was created. Worship was looked at with new eyes. Gradually the chapel began to flourish, younger members relying on older members in all kinds of ways, older members very aware that without the younger people they would no longer have a chapel at all.

It is often easier for a small church to make such changes. Participation in worship is less threatening than in a larger church. All age groups sharing together becomes a possibility in a way that could be far more difficult elsewhere. Of course, the disadvantage is that with a small number there are fewer people on whom to draw to implement change. This, in itself, may be no bad thing. It often gives opportunities to people who would never have considered that they had any active part to play in the preparation and conduct of worship. Of course, also, there are fewer people to oppose new ideas!

11 The Lord bless you and keep you . . .

Only one promise within the sacraments of the church is made by the whole community, acting and speaking together. This is the baptismal promise. The minister asks:

> Members of the Body of Christ, who are now in his name to receive this child, will you so maintain the common life of worship and service that s/he and all the children among you may grow in grace and in the knowledge and love of God and of his Son Jesus Christ our Lord?

© 1975 The Methodist Conference. Used by permission of Methodist Publishing House.

The congregation replies:

> With God's help we will.

It might seem that, of all the services which take place in church, a baptism is where young children should be most welcome. This is not always true. Of course, the child to be baptized and the parents are welcome, but other young children may be less so.

Brothers and sisters

The Baptismal service can be a very difficult occasion for older brothers and sisters of the child being baptized. They are often very young themselves, may not be used to being in church and may react to the strange environment in a number of ways. It is not unusual for brothers and sisters of two, three, four and five to be totally overwhelmed and to sob their way through the service. Equally, they sometimes jump up and down on the cushions round the communion rail, make determined efforts to somersault over the rail or make the most of being in an unfamiliarly large space and explore it at speed.

It is not surprising that the occasion is difficult, even if the older brothers and sisters are used to coming to church. In this sacramental act the small, smelly, demanding interloper in their family takes centre stage. The service reinforces all they have come to suspect, that they are no longer as important in the eyes of the adults around them, who are fascinated by the newcomer.

The minister and the church community can help these children feel that they are important in the eyes of God and of the church, that they are not bored or frustrated onlookers but have a part to play in the service. They could go forward with their parents. Perhaps they could hold the large-sized service book as the minister performs the baptism (when it often appears that the minister needs at least three hands!). With help they can receive the candle which is often given to the child being baptized, who is, almost invariably, too young to receive it. In churches where the minister takes newly-baptized children round the church to be introduced to the congregation, they can go too, to help in the introductions. Indeed, the whole family could take the child round, accompanied by the minister.

Other young children

But, what of the other young children present? These will probably include other young children in the baptismal party (who may or may not be used to coming to church) and the children of those who regularly attend the church. How can they be helped to join in, to worship in the way that is possible for them?

The Service

The Baptismal service involves participation in the form of responses, not only from the congregation, but, importantly, from the parents. It also involves the senses and the use of

The Lord bless you and keep you

Hadley Wood   *Paul Bateman (1954-)*

The Lord bless you and keep you: the Lord make his face to shine up-on you, and be gra-cious un-to you: the Lord lift up his coun-te-nance up-on you,___ and give you peace.

Music: © Paul Bateman   from Numbers 6:24-6 symbolism more fully than most acts of worship. All these elements combine to make it easier for people of all ages to share in worship together.

The music

Time was when the only hymn ever sung at baptisms (or so it seemed!) was 'See Israel's gentle Shepherd stand'. We now draw from a wider range of hymns, but it can be helpful to use one hymn regularly so that the children get to know it. Another possibility is to learn a musical setting of the words which are said by the whole congregation immediately following the baptism. (See page 51.)

Other factors

At a Baptismal service everyone wants to see what is going on. Adults crane their heads to look at the baby, delighting in smiles and gurgles, responding with concern (and sometimes amusement) to loud howls. But the only view for young children may be the backside of the person in front. Even if children stand on the seat (and not all seats are safe for this purpose) they are rarely any better off. One possibility is to invite young children to gather close to the font, with their parents if appropriate, in order to see what is going on and to be part of it.

The same provisions should be made for young children as at any other all-age service: a quiet place to play, toys to play with and so on. The nature of the service, however, is likely to create a higher level of interest and participation.

Some church members try to insist that the child who has been baptized, older brothers and sisters and visiting children should leave the service immediately after the baptism to join the other children of the church in separate age groups or the crèche. Some children may be happy to do this, but many will be overawed by the whole experience and need to stay with their parents for reassurance. This particularly applies to the older brothers and sisters of the child who has been baptized, who should not be 'sent out' while the baby 'stays in'. After all, what are they missing? What exciting things are happening in their absence? Why have they had their noses pushed out of joint again?

Some churches take photographs of children brought for baptism and keep them in a large album. This can be a great source of interest to young children, and, indeed, to older members. It may sometimes be appropriate for the minister to draw attention to the album, reminding younger and older members that they are all part of Christ's Church from the moment of baptism:

>'By baptism we receive this child into the congregation of Christ's flock...'

The Sacrament of Baptism has a central place in the life of the church and its people. It is vital that it should happen in such a way that people of all ages may begin to come to an awareness of its significance for them and for others.

12　The bread we break

'Why are most of the grown-ups kept in at the end of the service? What have they done wrong?' Such are the memories of an adult of his thoughts as a young child when the church members took part in the quarterly Communion Service.

Until recent years children were spectators, not participants, at Holy Communion. They were, in fact, rarely present, as the pattern from the middle of the nineteenth century was for them to attend Sunday School. It had not always been like this. John Wesley received Communion from the age of seven and his writings record occasions when he gave communion to children at his own services.

In the last few years, there has been a great development in the understanding of the place of children in the church. This has resulted from a new look at the attitude of Jesus towards children and new understandings of the place of children within families and communities. A recent Church of Scotland report stated:

> They (children) belong to the Church and the Church belongs to them. They are not only to be taught but to be ministered to; not only to be educated but to be nurtured; not only to learn but to worship; not only to receive but to give; truly to be part of today's Church.

The 1985 Methodist report on Christian Initiation said:

> Baptism is the one essential rite for entry into the Church and those who have received it are entitled to their place at the Lord's Table, though it may be expedient for this to be delayed.

Young children and Holy Communion

What about the very young and Holy Communion? In the last few years, practice has changed in the Methodist and United Reformed Churches and the Church of Scotland, to name three, to enable baptized children to receive the elements. The practice is increasing, though it is by no means universal.

Age limits

Some local churches impose age limits, but these can cause difficulties. The Methodist guidelines (issued in 1987) state:

> The Church Council should satisfy itself that the child shows an awareness of the significance of the Lord's Supper, and the faith response appropriate to the child's age and experience.

Increasingly ministers have found themselves saying, 'If children put out their hands to receive the elements what right have I to refuse them?' 'Would I refuse an adult with severe learning difficulties or Alzheimer's Disease on the basis of their limited understanding? If not these, why then young children?'

There have been some interesting examples:

- A three-year-old, having received Communion, spent a considerable time reverently placing individual glasses, which had been left haphazardly by the adults, into the holes provided.
- A father, knowing that his young child would not receive the elements, shared his bread with his child.
- A seven-year-old, who had received the elements while visiting a church on holiday, knowing that she would receive only a blessing from her local minister, took her own bread to church.
- A four-year-old, denied the bread and wine, whispered to her mother, 'I'm hungry too'.

The impact of Holy Communion on young children

Holy Communion has held a central place throughout the centuries. It is surely no coincidence that in this service all the senses come into play. Although we are all deeply influenced by our senses this is particularly true for young children. Do we wish to deprive our children of the service which is likely to have more influence on them than any other? Children have a great capacity to show awe and wonder. Do we take away from them the sacrament in which they will most fully be able to express this? Do we wish our young children to feel excluded at this, the most important act in the life of the church?

Factors to be considered

If young children are invited to share in Holy Communion there are certain factors to consider:

- The views of parents are crucial to any decision regarding their child.
- It is the responsibility of the church to provide a continuing learning programme to help people discover more about what they are doing.
- If children who have not been baptized wish to take Communion it should not be denied to them but conversations should begin with parents concerning the possibility of Baptism.

There are also practical steps which can be taken regarding the service.

- An illustrated version of *The Sunday Service* is available.
- Young children enjoy repetition and can cope with difficult words if they are repeated so that they get to know them.
- There is a case for the occasional use of a different, simpler form.

    Some Communion hymns are particularly suitable when young children are present. These include 'As your family, Lord' (HP595), 'Let us break bread together' (HP615) and 'Jesus the Lord said "I am the Bread"' (HP137). (See also page 58.)

Children who participate in Holy Communion from a young age will have the opportunity to grow through their experiences to a commitment and acceptance of their responsibilities at the time of Confirmation.

In recent years many churches have found that the service of Holy Communion is the one where, above all, it is possible to have a truly all-age celebration.

Eat This Bread

Ostinato Response - Mixed Voices

Music: J. Berthier

♩ = 80 Meditative

Eat this bread, drink this cup, come to me and never be hungry.
Eat this bread, drink this cup, trust in me and you will not thirst.

© Ateliers et Presses de Taizé, 71250 Taizé communaute, France.

13 The Kingdom of God belongs to such as these

I was telling a group of five and six year olds a story about a real mouse and a clockwork mouse. The real mouse wanted to change places because the little girl who lived at his house was frightened of him, but liked the clockwork mouse. After certain adventures the story ended with the real mouse finding the clockwork mouse on a rubbish tip. The little girl had had a birthday and a pile of new toys. The clockwork mouse had been rejected.

I asked the children in what ways it would be better to be a robot than a child. There were many ideas, such as: 'You wouldn't have to go to school', 'You wouldn't have to wash', 'You wouldn't have to do what your mum said'. Then Christopher made his contribution: 'You would never die', he said. I then asked the children in what ways it was better to be a child than a robot. Again, there were many ideas: 'You can go on holiday', 'You can go to McDonalds for a hamburger'. But again, finally, Christopher came into the picture: 'You can choose', he said.

Young children bring many things to worship. They bring enthusiasm, a love of the natural world, a sense of awe and wonder, creativity, freshness, open-ness – the list goes on and on. But perhaps we underestimate their ability to think and to understand. We do not listen to them as often as we should and therefore we do not really know what they are saying and thinking. As a result we often do not know where to begin.

Above all, young children bring themselves. It would be unthinkable to celebrate Christmas without the youngest members of the family. After all, they are important people at Christmas, when we celebrate God's coming to earth as a tiny child. In the same way it should surely be unthinkable never to allow them to share in worship with the whole church community. Are they not always important members of our community?

14 Resources

Children at Holy Communion, MDEY, 1988

First Steps in the Church, MDEY, 1992

Splash, Scripture Union, 1992

Praying with Sticky Fingers, MDEY, 1992

Milestones, MDEY, 1993

Under Fives Welcome, Scripture Union, 1990

First Steps, Church House Publishing, 1987

How Faith Grows, National Society/CHP, 1991

Children in the Way, National Society/CHP, 1988

The Spiritual Life of Children, Harper/Collins, 1992

God-Talk with Young Children, CEM, 1991

Going to Church with Children, Joint Board of Christian Education, Melbourne, 1987

Roots and Wings, MDEY; 1994:
- Caring for Under Fives
- Crèches
- Pram Services
- Toddlers' Groups

Praise, A J McCallen Collins Liturgical, 1979

Noah's Ark, Bride Adams-Ray, The Grail, England, 1981

The Selfish Giant, Oscar Wilde, Neugebauer Press, 1984

The Little Gate, Mike Butterworth and Mick Inkpen (and others in this series), Marshall Morgan and Scott, 1989

Badger's Parting Gifts, Susan Varley, Picture Lions, 1985

The Clown of God, Tomie de Paolo, Methuen, 1985

The Velveteen Rabbit, Margery Williams, Heinemann, 1983

Story Song, Stainer & Bell/MDEY, 1993

Sent by the Lord, Iona, 1991

Many and Great, Iona, 1990

Celtic prayers by David Adam:

The Edge of Glory, Triangle/SPCK, 1985
Tides and Seasons, Triangle/SPCK, 1989
Border Lands, SPCK, 1991